Flying Machines and Their Heroes

THE PISTON WARRIORS OF WWII

BY
Errol Kennedy

First edition 2015
Published by Lundarien Press, UK
Copyright © Errol Kennedy & Imagination Band Ltd 2015

ISBN 978-1-910816-37-0

The right of Errol Kennedy to be identified as the author of this work has been asserted in accordance with the Copyright, Designs and Patents Act 1988

For more info and other books in this series, including this audiobook read by Shane Rimmer & Ashley Slater, go to:

flyingmachinesandtheirheroes.com

Other Books in the
Flying Machines and Their Heroes Series

1. THE BLENHEIM BOMBER STORY

2. AGAINST ALL ODDS - The Guinea Pig Story

3. BY DAY AND BY NIGHT - The B17 and Lancaster Bomber Story

4. TWO LEGENDS OF WWII - Spitfire and Mustang Story

...more to follow soon

Contents

The Piston Warriors of WWII Story   7

Appendix 1 - The Royal Auxiliary Air Force   57
Appendix 2 - The Second World War   60

THE PISTON WARRIORS OF WWII

In 1939 the shadow of war loomed over the world stage for the second time this century. It was a prelude to the darkest and most destructive chapter in the history of mankind, the Second World War. It proved to be more costly in both human terms and resources than any other conflict known to mankind, eclipsing even the carnage of the Great War. The cause and effect of this intensive period of conflict even up until this very day has profoundly affected the world we live in. The people who lived and fought through the period would never again capture the intense feelings and experiences they endured, the fear, the courage, the loss and the intensity of life, the opportunity to fight for strong convictions had never before been more apparent.

Many countries fought the war on their own soil, the rest rallied to their aid offering resources and manpower and if necessary their lives for their belief in freedom and self-determination. The early days saw the optimism of "it will all be over by Christmas" but the reality was six long years of destruction and bloodshed that reached virtually every corner of the globe.

Huge battles were fought, some were won, some lost, but all of them contributed to the eventual downfall of the Axis forces. In those early dark months one nation stood alone against Germany's might, Great Britain. The responsibilities for keeping the invaders out of the Island fortress fell on the Royal Air Force after the army's defeat at Dunkirk where the fields and beaches now lay waste to the aftermath of a bloody battle. The RAF rose magnificently to the challenge during the Battle of Britain.

For the time being at least, Britain was safe but she sorely needed the help of her mighty cousin across the pond, the United States of America. The huge resources and courage of the colossus were brought to bear after the Japanese attacked Pearl Harbour in 1941.

America, that champion of freedom and democracy was on the warpath. At last the RAF had found a true partner, the mightiest air force in the world. Together they would bring about the defeat of Germany and Japan. That partnership exists even today and as the events of the Gulf War have proved, the United States Air Force and the Royal Air Force are invincible.

By 1940, Britain stood alone; France, Belgium and Holland had fallen to the mighty German jackboot. Hitler stood on the French coast and looked across at the White Cliffs of Dover.

It was only a matter of time before Britain would be invaded. Chamberlain's government had toppled and Winston Churchill was the new Prime Minister.

For a long time Churchill had been aware of the imminent danger of a massive air attack from the Luftwaffe. In a speech to the nation he decreed that, "the battle of France is over, I fear that the battle of Britain is about to begin."

This fear was soon realised when the phoney war came to and end in the early months of 1940. The RAF were losing men and machines at an alarming rate over the Channel and France, resources and morale were at a low ebb. Britain desperately needed an ally if it was to hold off an invasion. Churchill wooed Roosevelt and the American nation into helping the beleaguered island but the American people were not ready to go to war. By the summer of 1940 it was becoming desperate, Dowding's men of Fighter Command were flying eighteen hours a day, landing only to refuel and rearm. Fighter Command had only 470 serviceable aircraft against the might of the Luftwaffe's 2000. Hitler knew full well that if an attack on England was to succeed, it had to be in the summer and before mounting his land operation he first had to defeat the RAF.

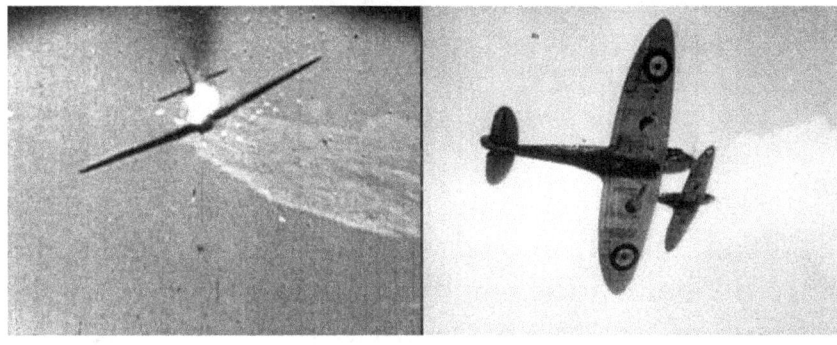

By July Hitler's troops were ready. Operation Sea Lion, the invasion of Britain, was about to begin. Hundreds of barges were prepared for the crossing and hundreds of thousands of Nazi troops lined the European coastline looking westward. Britain held her breath in anticipation of the fight. The war in the skies raged over England during July and August, the RAF fought relentlessly.

Goring had assured Hitler of the Luftwaffe's air superiority over British skies. However, he had not taken into account the sheer tenacity and doggedness of Britain's young pilots.

The Luftwaffe tried desperately to knock out the RAF on the ground, destroying the airfields and aircraft before they had a chance to get airborne. Unknown to the German's they were slowly succeeding. But then came Hitler's big mistake. Unaware that he was actually making progress in the battle he switched tactics, instead of sending the Luftwaffe to bomb the airfields he turned his bombs on London believing that this would break the British spirit. This was the reprieve the RAF had been waiting for. They now had time to regroup and rearm concentrating all of their fighter squadrons into the South of England in preparation for the invasion.

Hitler, after two previous postponements planned his invasion for the 15th September and by 11.00 hours a massive formation of German aircraft were sighted over the English Channel. The Battle of Britain was now in its final phase. The RAF put up every fighter they could muster being outnumbered 5 to 1 they locked horns with the Luftwaffe. The Germans had believed that they had broken the RAF's ability to fight and were convinced that the inventory of aircraft was now down to a mere handful. Yet to the surprise of the German pilots, fighter after fighter ripped into their formations creating havoc, causing heavy losses.

For the first time in the war the Luftwaffe had met its match. At last German invincibility was being questioned; Goring's Luftwaffe was turned around and defeated.

By September 17th Hitler had abandoned his plans to invade England and his troops pulled back into France. The Battle of Britain was a victory for the RAF and the first major blow inflicted on the mighty German war machine.

Those famous words of Winston Churchill have

forever immortalised those brave young fighter pilots.

He said in emotion: *"Never in the field of human conflict was so much owed by so many to so few."*

The Supermarine Spitfire was more than just a successful fighter; it was the material symbol of final victory to the British people in their darkest hour and it its one of the only RAF fighters of the Second World War to achieve a truly legendary status.

Certainly no other fighter is more deserving in its

place among the famous. In over 40 different variants since its conception, built in greater numbers than any British aircraft, it flew operationally on every front between 1939 and 1945 and it was engaged in every major air action fought by the RAF at that time.

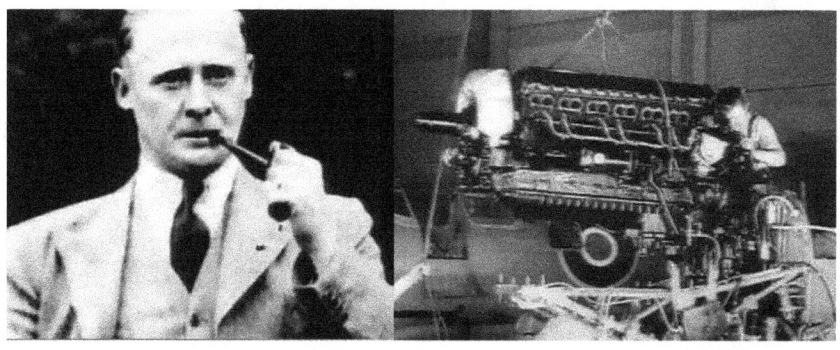

Designed by Mitchell, one of Britain's most brilliant designers and powered by the famous Rolls Royce Merlin engine the success which attended the Spitfire from even its earliest days, was no accident. Like any truly great aircraft, the Spitfire was both an inspired design and the outcome of a lengthy process of technical development. From the beginning to the end of the war the Spitfire was in the forefront of the fighting.

They fought over the beaches of Dunkirk and above the D-Day landings four years later. They supported the Fourteenth Army in Burma, they took part in the invasion of Greece. In 1943 they repulsed Japanese attacks on Darwin Australia, they flew in the Solomon Islands, Borneo and New Guinea. In fact the Spitfire operated everywhere the RAF was committed and was flown at one time or another by nearly all the RAF's leading wartime fighter pilots.

It was paid many tributes by friend and foe alike but perhaps one of the greatest came from Germany's General Galland when he was asked for his fighter requirements by Reich Marshall Goring, he answered, "I should like a squadron of Spitfires." More than 22,000 Spitfires were built, no other combat aircraft has better served its country and they were undoubtedly the one truly immortal aeroplane to emerge from the Second World War.

If the Spitfire was the star of the Battle of Britain, the Hawker Hurricane was definitely the workhorse.

The Hurricane was the first fighter monoplane to join the RAF and the first RAF fighter capable of speeds over 300 mph at level flight. Designed by Sydney Camm and powered by Rolls Royce engines, on later variants; the Merlin engine, the Hurricane was largely responsible for the successful outcome of the Battle of Britain.

They shouldered the lion's share of Britain's defence with more than three fifths of the RAF's Fighter Command being Hurricane squadrons. The Hurricane also proved to possess an amazing propensity for adaption and the multi-purpose roles that it performed earned for it the distinction of being the most versatile of single seat warplanes to emerge from the Second World War.

Although the Hurricane and Spitfire shared an immortal partnership and were briefly built to the same requirements, they represented entirely different approaches to the same problem. The wood and canvas construction of the Hurricane was based on the logical outcome of a long line of fighting aircraft, whereas the metal Spitfire was an entirely new concept based on specialised experience. The Hurricane was workmanlike, rugged and sturdy, the Spitfire slender and ballerina-like. One was the studied application of experience, the other a stroke of genius.

Although inferior in performance to its German counterparts, the Hurricane, proved itself more than capable in combat by virtue of its superb manoeuvrability. It could take a remarkable amount of punishment and had several outstanding qualities. If offered a good view for the pilot, it was less sensitive to excessive approach speeds than the Spitfire and its wide track undercarriage allowed greater liberties to be taken while landing. 14,000 Hurricanes were built; its versatility is unlikely to ever be surpassed by any other combat aircraft.

In 1936 when the Blenheim had made its debut, it was immediately hailed as a major step forward in combat aircraft design. It was the RAF's first all metal monoplane of stressed skin construction and as such it denoted a new era for the Royal Air Force. More than any other, the Blenheim sounded the end of the line for the fighting biplane.

When the war came, the Blenheim was the first aeroplane used in combat by the Royal Air Force and very soon it became the backbone of the RAF's bomber command. Later on in their war career they were fitted with a new operational fighter radar system thus converting them to a fighter configuration.

At the time the Blenheim was both praised and abused and although it was woefully vulnerable as a bomber to fighter attacks it was all that was available to the RAF. While the exploits of the Blenheim during wartime were overshadowed by other more famous aeroplanes, this aircraft made a significant contribution to the development of the RAF. The Blenheim was one of the aircraft on which bomber command cut its teeth, with it the RAF learned a great deal about the daylight operations over enemy territory. Thus the Blenheim perhaps not the most effective of weapons is still deserving in its place amongst the significant aircraft of World War II and in the history of the RAF.

By1941 the question was not, if the United States would join in the war raging in Europe, but when. They were doing everything they could to help their beleaguered cousins falling short only in an outright declaration of war. Supplies flowed across the Atlantic in convoys and the newly elected President Roosevelt, warned America that the fight for freedom was also the responsibility of the American people. He started to mobilise the American nation into war production.

The United States Air Forces were given a two-year expansion plan combining the forces into one unit; the United States Army Air Forces. Manpower was increased from

9,000 to 140,000 and the inventory of serviceable aircraft stood at over 6,000.

The land lease agreement was signed which allowed both Britain and China supplies, machinery and weaponry to be paid for in kind after the war. This agreement provoked the Japanese nation; they demanded an outright cessation of aid to China. The German's were also provoked by the agreement; they subsequently began attacking US shipping indiscriminately. Then the Japanese entered the war by invading South Indochina. The Americans were outraged by this active aggression and froze all Japanese assets in the United States. The Japanese in response to this, warned America that Japan would be fully ready for war by October 1941. Throughout the world, war was now spreading.

On the 26th November 1941 the United States Government demanded immediate Japanese withdrawal from Indochina or they would suffer the consequences. On the very same day the Japanese fleet set sail.

Before 1941 came to a close the people of the United States were dealt a violent blow. Britain was soon to have the allies she so desperately needed. In fact, Winston Churchill's prayers were about to be answered.

The Islands of Hawaii seemed to be so far away from the clutches of the war in Europe, yet on the morning of December 7th, Japanese fighters were droning their way towards the Islands of Hawaii, their destination, the US naval base at Pearl

Harbour. All ships had returned to port having just completed exercises during the previous week apart from the carriers Lexington and Enterprise, which had left the day before on route to the Midway Islands.

On the surrounding airfields the aircraft stood on neat rows on the tarmac, it was a peaceful sunny Sunday morning. The only airborne traffic was the expected arrival of a flight of B17's coming in from America. The Japanese had calculated that this was the perfect time to surprise their victim and they were right. Surprise was complete.

At 07.50 hrs the first waive of Japanese aircraft appeared over Pearl Harbour, launching torpedo's at the serried ranks of warships in Battleship Row.

Simultaneously they attacked the airfield at Wheeler Field, Kaneohe, Ewa and Hickam. The surprise was complete. They had managed to destroy a large part of the US fleet; the aircraft lay waste across the airfields.

The flight of B17's coming in from the US were also destroyed. They were unarmed to save weight on their long flight and were totally defenceless against the waive of Zero's that bore down on them.

A second waive of aircraft appeared one hour later but this time the US defences were a little more prepared.

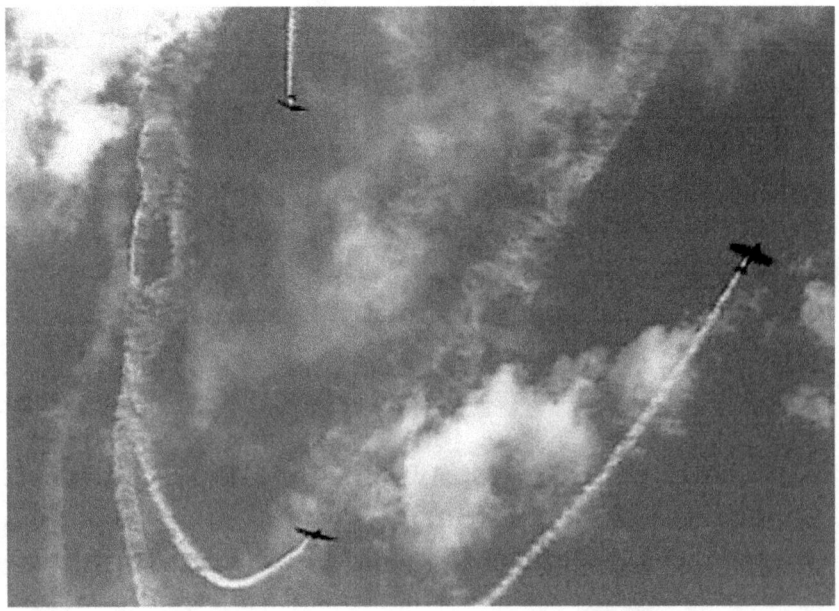

Nevertheless they caused even more carnage and wrecked three more destroyers and one battleship. By 10 o'clock it was all over. The US fleet had been all but wiped out; 63 aircraft had been totally destroyed and the United States was now at war.

One of the American fighters that managed to get airborne during the attack and fight back was the Curtis P40.

The P40, previously designated the P36, was undoubtedly one of the most controversial fighters to serve in quantity during World War II, loved by some pilots and hated by others. Yet as the first single-seater fighter to go into mass production for the US Air Force, it subsequently bore much of the brunt of air warfare over several battlefronts.

Although its performance was not great, its sturdiness and ability to take exceeding amounts of flak and punishment made up for any of its shortfalls. It was amenable to adaptation; more important it was always serviceable when needed. Along with the Bell Air Cobra the P40 made up more than half of the strength of all USAAF fighters at the time. Because of its low altitude flying capabilities and rugged construction, the P40 proved to be an excellent ground attack weapon.

They served in almost every theatre of war including service with the Royal Air Force where it was named the Tomahawk, serving mainly in the Middle East and North Africa, although some were used in England. One of the most famous configuration of P40's was with the American Volunteer Group fighting in China; the Flying Tigers. The P40 underwent many changes in its variant including the Mohawk, the Tomahawk, the Kittyhawk and the Warhawk. Later variants were fitted with a Packard Merlin engine which increased speed to over 370 mph. Good, bad or indifferent, the P40 was the only capable fighter the USAAF had when it went to war. More than 14,000 were delivered during those years and will always be remembered by the majority of its pilots who viewed it with affection. Most pilots have affection for one aircraft or another, very few equal the sheer numbers of pilots from the United States who hold a great affection for one aircraft in particular, probably the first combat aircraft they ever flew in, the advance trainer, the North American Texan.

Although not truly a combat aircraft, the Texan deserves as much credit in the annals of aviation history as any other for it was this aircraft that gave those brave US pilots and some RAF pilots the training and experience that no doubt saved their lives on endless occasions. The USAAF had been born into a world of rapid expansion plans in both man and machine. This resulted in thousands of new men being trained to fly practically overnight.

The Texan was the key aircraft that was going to

make this expansion plan possible and would become the keystone of the USAAF. Also known as the Harvard to the RAF pilots and the Yale to the Canadians, the early Texans were built of plywood construction in order to preserve valuable aluminium resources for the construction of combat aircraft. She was capable of speeds over 200 mph with a maximum range of 750 miles powered by a 600 horsepower Pratt & Whitney engine.

Although most of the Texans were armed for training purposes, some actually saw combat duty. Dependability and durability being only two of its assets, the aeroplane saw service in almost every theatre of war, being easy to maintain and repair the Texan could do anything a fighter could do only perhaps not quite as quickly. Designed to give the best possible training in all types of tactics, from ground bombardment to aerial dog fighting the Texan was possibly the best trainer aircraft in the world. They carried such versatile equipment as bomb racks, blind flying instrumentation, gun and standard cameras, fixed and flexible guns and just about every device that a pilot would have to operate in combat.

The Texan has been called by many the most universally used aeroplane in history. That may be an exaggeration; she was definitely the most universally used trainer ever built and was undoubtedly one of the USAAF's most important acquisitions during the war years.

The Texan wasn't the only aeroplane supplied and built by North American; it was one of the USAAF's important acquisitions. To fill a requirement later in the war for a fighter that could fly long range, giving the bombers much needed support, North American designers produced an aeroplane that could only rank alongside the RAF Spitfire as being one of the most superior fighters of World War II; the P-51 Mustang.

The P-51, undoubtedly the finest of all American wartime fighters, outperforming all in its class in terms of speed, range and manoeuvrability, was conceived almost by accident. In fact, the Mustang owed much of its origin to the British Air Purchasing Commission, which in April 1940 requested a substitute for the Curtis P40, which was becoming unsuitable for European combat situations. North American Aviation were consulted and felt they could offer better than a revamped P40.

This resulted in the prototype Mustang being produced in only 117 days. As soon as the first production Mustangs arrived in England, they were immediately recognised as being outstandingly superior to any other American fighter type. Development then brought out the addition of a new Merlin engine. When the USAAF eventually took delivery of Mustangs in 1943, the aeroplane really came into its own and also came as a shock to the Luftwaffe, they had posed a serious threat to German defences when they accompanied the B17's and liberators all the way to Berlin and back.

The great American test pilot, Chuck Yeager, flew the Mustang all over Europe during the conflict and called it the best American fighter in the war and equal to anything the German's could throw at it. He ought to have known, for in 1944 he scored five of his aerial victories in one day alone flying a Mustang.

Goring also paid tribute to the Mustang when he admitted privately that he had realised that Germany would lose the war when he saw the P-51's over Germany. Throughout the war the production of Mustangs moved at a rapid rate increasing the fighter strength of the USAAF in Europe, Italy, China and in the Pacific where they soon proved to be a match for the infamous Japanese Zero. They also become a match for the jet-propelled Messerschmitt 262 that became operational in 1944. Although the jet enemy was faster, the Mustang had the edge in terms of manoeuvrability. The Mustang ended the war as the cream of the USAAF fighters, if not the top fighter of the war.

Nearly half of all enemy aircraft shot down over Europe were accredited to Mustangs, while in the Pacific they controlled the skies over the Japanese homelands. When the Mustang was finally retired in 1957 this wonderful aeroplane that had almost been conceived by mistake had become a legend.

With the world now at war the bond between the RAF and the USAAF became even greater. The US continued to send aircraft and aircrew to England to support the war in Europe and RAF pilots were being trained in the United States. Whilst Europe was considered as the most important theatre of war with regard to an early victory and almost every other front the allied air forces were prominent as comrades in arms. Supported by the Royal Air Forces of Australia, New Zealand, Canada and India, the RAF and the USAAF fought it out over North Africa, India, China, the Middle East and Indochina.

The RAF attacked the Luftwaffe over Norway whilst the US concentrated secondary attacks on the Japanese over the Pacific Islands. Development in new aircraft and air warfare was progressing at an outstanding rate. The dark days were over and it was now only a matter of time before the allied powers would have total supremacy over the world. The German occupied areas were shrinking fast as the allies put the pressure on from the south and the west, whilst the Russians pushed them back mercilessly from the east. The Japanese empire had control of thousands of islands in the Pacific, regaining these islands was taking a terrible toll on young American and Commonwealth lives. The Japanese fought relentlessly.

Named after William Mitchell, the farsighted crusading American Colonel of the 1920's who was court marshalled on his outspoken views on air power, the North American B25 was possibly the best all round light medium bomber of the Second

World War. Operationally efficient, this docile adaptable machine had an excellent all round performance with particularly good handling characteristics and it was one of the most popular of combat aircraft among all the allied aircrews. Had the Mitchell never attacked another objective, it would still have ranked among the most truly significant and historic aircraft of the war for its fantastic attack against Tokyo in 1942 when it operated from the flight deck of the USSS Hornet on the famous "Doolittle Raid." This was the very first attack on the Japanese mainland and although its primary importance was symbolic it also represented one of the most remarkable achievements of air combat in the war.

The American Government after the attack on Pearl Harbour, came up with an almost absurd plan of retaliation, they wanted to bomb Japan immediately. The problem was that no US bomber had the range necessary and normal carrier based planes could not get near enough without coming under attack from Japanese patrols. The B25 was considered as the best aircraft for the job, being able to take off from a carrier just outside patrol range. On April 18th after weeks of practice, sixteen B25's led by Colonel Jimmy Doolittle, managed to take off from the carrier USSS Hornet. All sixteen aircraft reached their target and dropped their bomb loads.

This one raid resulted in a massive positive boost to the US morale and had a severe negative effect on the Japanese. During its wartime service the B25 made its mark on almost every front of the war. It was manufactured in larger quantities than any other American twin-engine bomber, many of them also seeing 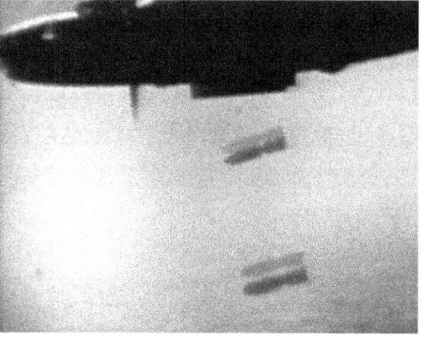 service with the Royal Air Forces and other Allied Air Forces. In its multitude of variants the B25 saw action right up until the end of the war on every battlefront.

The Mitchell built up an unrivalled tradition of service. There can be few more dramatic examples of the constant development of a basic design under the period of war than offered by this remarkable aircraft.

One of the main USAAF fighters in the Pacific; was the Lockheed Lightning or the "fork tailed devil" as it became known to the Japanese and Germans alike.

Although the Lightning was produced in smaller numbers than any other USAAF fighter, it still served on every battle front in a wide variety of roles ranging from fighter bombing, to casualty evacuation and smoke laying. If slightly slower and less manoeuvrable than the Mustang and the Thunderbolt, the Lightning offered the advantage of twin-engine operation, which with its added safety factor had an excellent combat range. The

Lightning brought many firsts for the USAAF apart from being Lockheed's first military aircraft.

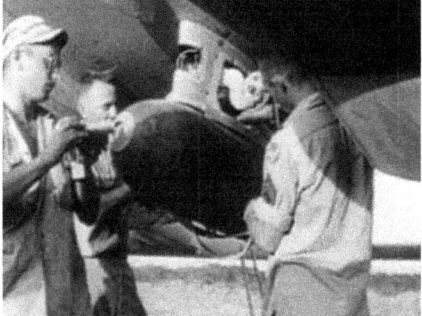

It was the first fighter with twin turbo super chargers, the first USAAF twin boom aircraft and the first twin-engine single seat fighter used by that force.

The Lightning was designed to meet a requirement in 1937 for a high altitude interceptor with a maximum speed of at least 360 mph at 20,000 feet and 290 mph at sea level. It also had to be able to take off and land over a 50 feet obstacle within 2,200 feet. By the spring of 1944 there were thirteen P38 Lightning groups in overseas operational units with the USAAF. In Europe, serving with the 9th Air Force, they operated on long-range fighter escort and ground attack duties.

While in the Pacific they were at the forefront of the island hopping campaign where they claimed more Japanese fighters destroyed than any other fighter.

The World War II Ace, the late Major Richard Bond scored all forty of his victories in a P38 Lightning in the Pacific closely followed by another Lightning pilot, Major Thomas McGuire, who scored thirty-eight victories. In most parts, the Lightning was either liked or disliked by its pilots and the strong feelings fore and against the type raged throughout the war, perhaps making it one of the most controversial aircraft of the period. It was certainly less forgiving to inexperienced pilots but it proved undeniably that placed in the right hands, it was an excellent aircraft with a high altitude interception role for which it was designed.

The consolidated PBY Flying Boat, used by the US Navy, was also in service with the RAF, it was named the Catalina.

The Catalina was one of the best aircraft of its type during World War II. With its range of over 4,000 miles the Catalina proved a boom in protecting shipping convoys in the East Atlantic. 3300 Catalina's were built in the US and Canada during the war. Many more were built under licence in Russia.

These figures made it the largest production number of flying boats of all time. With two Victoria Crosses being awarded to Catalina pilots, the aircraft proved to be admirable with excellent range characteristics, good cruising performance and more importantly during times of war, a powerful offensive armament.

Coastal Commands equipment was a varied mixture of aircraft types including many from the US. One of the workhorses was the Avro Anson general reconnaissance. The Anson was used to patrol the North Sea through which German navel warships and submarines had to travel to reach the open ocean. Entering the service in 1936 the Anson was an old lady by the time the war came around. It was the first aircraft to be used by the RAF with a retractable undercarriage, although this involved no less than 122 turns of a hand operated cranking system.

The Anson entered the war with twelve squadrons of coastal command engaged mainly on reconnaissance and convoy escort missions.

Another aircraft that was used to train pilots, navigators and air gunners was the USAAF's Beach AT11, popularly known as the "Twin Beach"

With a bomb bay carrying ten 100lb bombs and equipped with a .30 calibre machine gun in its dorsal turret, it served as a bombardier and gunnery trainer. The AT7 version was a navigational trainer.

There was also a cargo version of this type, which was known as the C-45 Expeditor. The Twin Beach was one of the most successful and widely used aircraft of its size and type ever built. Many Twin Beach's were used after the war as corporate transport planes.

In February 1942 a new force entered the war in Europe; Bomber Harris, the Chief of the RAF's Bomber Command. Air Marshall Harris struck against the Luftwaffe's air superiority, the tactic was to launch a thousand bomber raids over the industrial towns and cities of Germany in an attempt to stem the German war machine and break the spirit of the German nation. Using every available operational aircraft, these massive formations flew at night bombing the very heart of Germany.

Meanwhile, the United States poured man and machines into England establishing bases from Lincolnshire to Gloucestershire. The 8th Air Force was concentrating on raiding smaller strategic targets by daylight. At the Casablanca Conference in 1943 it was decided between Roosevelt and Churchill that there was to be a combined bomber offensive against Germany and for the first time American bombs would be dropped on German soil. The idea of Operation Point Blank was to bomb the devils around the clock, the USAAF by day and the RAF by night. With the eastern front well established after the invasion of Russia, the German war machine was now stretched to capacity. The direct objective was to disrupt the Germanic war effort as much as possible and to lower morale in preparation for a combined cross channel allied attack.

One of the RAF's early bombers was the Vickers Wellington.

Blooded in combat in the very outset of hostilities, it carried the lion share of the RAF Bomber Command's night bombing offensive until the debut of the first four-engine bombers. It was still in front line offensives when the war ended.

Indeed such was the brilliant war record of the Wellington that any tribute can only be a pale reflection of the distinctions that this remarkable aircraft won for itself. The Wellington's docility combined with a lively performance and its ability to absorb an incredible amount of battle damage rapidly endeared it to its crews; its portly, well-fed appearance earned the name "Whippy" after Pop Eye's fat friend.

The Wellington was an aircraft worthy of the RAF bearing the distinction of the name of one of Britain's great soldiers. Many other bombers came forward as the war progressed but none earned a finer reputation.

Few other aircraft of the Second World War gained the universal affection of their aircrew over so long an operational period as the Boeing B17 Fortress, which formed the spearhead of the American bombing offensive in Europe from the beginning to the end. The Fortress also served in every other theatre of war. No other single aircraft type contributed more to the defeat of the Luftwaffe both in the air and on the ground than the B17.

The Fortress achieved fame on the strength of several outstanding attributes. Of these, perhaps the most important, were an excellent high altitude capability and the ability to absorb a staggering amount of battle damage. To these attributes were added an exceptionally heavy defensive armament, though the true combat potential of the Fortress was achieved only after a long period of gestation.

The Fortress dropped no less than 640,000 tons of bombs on European targets during the war years and according to records, the Fortress destroyed twenty-three enemy aircraft per thousand sorties.

Although the success rate of the B17 was high, there were appalling losses. It was a large aircraft, an easy target for the Luftwaffe. Machine gun fire with its convoluted construction the B17 could take, but rockets and cannon shells went through it like butter. When the Luftwaffe had fighter construction up to a thousand a month in 1943, they hit the B17 raids hard. In four months the USAAF lost 120% of its compliment of Fortresses. A bomber crew's tour had been raised to twenty-five missions with one in ten B17's being shot down on every mission, the crews were on borrowed time if they lasted after the first ten. Nevertheless by its almost unrivalled period of frontline service, the Fortress proved itself as one of the classic bombers of all time.

Its performance proved a triumphant vindication of the principles of air strategy and bomber design established by the far-sighted airmen and engineers of the USA long before World War II.

Many aircraft employed during the war became famous, few were truly great. On a par with the USAAF's B17 was the RAF's Avro Lancaster.

Greatness is a quality which cannot be installed in an aircraft on the drawing board or on the assembly line. A great aircraft must have that touch of genius which transcends the good and it must have luck, the luck to be in the right place at the right time. It must have flying qualities well above average, reliability, ruggedness and fighting ability and in the final analysis it needs the skilled touch of crews to which it has endeared itself.

As with the Fortress, the Spitfire and Mustang before it, the Lancaster had all these in good measure. This four-engine bomber embodied a measure of grace which made it pleasing to the eye and it's neat aerodynamic shape contributed materially to its all round excellent performance.

Like so many good aircraft, the essence of this design was its simplicity; its robust structure being ideally suited for mass production and this was undoubtedly one of the main factors in its success. The Lancaster was also a remarkably adaptable and superlative bomber on every count and of all the great aircraft which fought throughout the war there are many who would insist that this was the greatest.

One of the most famous raids attributed to the Lancaster was that of 617 Squadron when nineteen crews set out to raid the Mohne and Eder Dams. The Dam Busters as they later became known, wrecked in that one mission no less than one hundred factories along the Ruhr Valley costing the German war machine dearly but the losses were high with eight aircraft and their crews lost in action.

Like old soldiers good aeroplanes never die, the Lancaster served with the RAF for long after the war. Bomber Harris praised the aircraft when he called it "the finest bomber of the war". The Lancaster far surpassed other types of heavy bombers in Europe. Not only could it take heavier bomb loads, not only was it easier to handle, and not only were there fewer accidents with this than any other type but the casualty rate was also well below any other four-engine bomber of the war. She was truly the greatest and most successful of Britain's bombers and she takes pride of place in the annals of the Royal Air Force.

Every aircraft has its staunch supporters but when it comes to fame, perhaps some become overshadowed. The consolidated Liberator lost out in terms of fame to the Boeing B17 but not in achievement. The Liberator was built in much larger numbers than the Fortress; in fact it was built in greater quantities than any other American aircraft.

Such a unique production record is all the more remarkable for it was such a large four-engine aircraft.

The Liberator operated for a longer period on operational fronts and was produced in a greater variety of versions than any other allied or enemy bomber. It did not carry the bomb load of the

Fortress but it did have distinct aerodynamic advantages including better overall performance, easier take-off and landing ability.

One of their prime virtues, and one which often hallmarks a great aeroplane, was its versatility. In addition to strategic bombing it was used with equal facility for maritime reconnaissance, antisubmarine operations, passenger and freight transportation, as a flying tanker and for photographic reconnaissance as well as for many other duties.

One of the more notable raids of the Liberator during the war was on the Ploesti Oilfields but despite vast damage to the targets the losses to the USAAF were catastrophic.

This was one of the first of the USAAF's strategic bombing operations and one which was to highlight the need for long range fighter escorts on daylight raids, which took a heavy toll on the brave B17 and B24 crews. Apart from its unrivalled production record, the liberator also earned for itself a permanent place in aviation history for it's remarkable record of achievement. Whether the load delivered happened to be bombs, depth charges, gasoline freight, troops or VIPs, the Liberator earned for itself the reputation which was second to none, for doing almost any job, anywhere.

Many of the world's greatest combat aircraft had been born not as a result of some officially inspired specification, but because of the unshakable conviction of a man or of a group of individuals with a revolutionary idea.

Few better examples could be cited than that of the DeHavilland Mosquito which diverged so far from the official views pertaining at that time of it's conception, that it came precariously close to being scrapped before it was born. It was the

DeHavilland Company alone and their belief in a bomber that could outpace any intercepting fighter that gave the RAF one of their most potent weapons of the Second World War. The result was a performance which far surpassed that of any other aircraft available to the combatants between 1941 and 1944. As with other great aircraft, the Mosquito's attributes included its versatility which as the war progressed, earned it the accolade of being all things to all men.

On the 6th August 1945, one Colonel Paul Tibbits took off from the Tinian Island in the Pacific in a Boeing B29 Super Fortress with an eleven-man crew accompanied by two other B29's. Colonel Tibbits had been flying special missions over the Japanese Islands in preparation for this one raid. The modified aircraft on this mission had its insignia painted out, replaced instead with classified victory numbers.

Tibbits' crew were aware that they were carrying an awesome new weapon in the bomb bay but they were unaware of its precise nature; it was a cylindrical devise weighing almost 10,000 lbs and containing 140 lbs of deadly uranium 235. The bomb was codenamed "Little Boy", the atom bomb, the target for the mission, Hiroshima. The bomb load was released over its target at 09.15 hrs at an altitude of 31,600 feet. Little Boy exploded 800 feet above the target with the equivalent force of 20,000 tons of TNT. Colonel Tibbits pulled the aircraft into a 150-degree turn to escape the glare and the blast. This mission was going to wreak havoc on the Japanese nation and what followed caused the history books to be closed on World War II forever.

The damage to the target was unprecedented, some four and a half square miles of the city and 48,000 buildings were destroyed, 78,000 people were killed and another 51,000 were seriously injured. The world had never before seen carnage on such a scale and awaited the reaction from Japan. It wasn't forthcoming, the Japanese remained silent.

Three days later a second bomb again from a B29 was released over its target Nagasaki, another 35,000 people were killed in the configuration. Five days later Japan surrendered, the war was over.

While the Super Fortress gained for itself undying fame as the first aircraft to drop an atomic weapon, it also earned for itself a place in the history of aerial warfare against Japan.

The Super Fortress proved beyond doubt that strategic bombing could win wars by neutralising the enemy's industrial and military capabilities. The war was over leaving the United States and Britain with a colossal combined air force. This was obviously an impractical situation for the years of peace which everybody hoped would stretch ahead. Many squadrons were disbanded, aircraft were scrapped but the USAAF and the RAF were to achieve one more major show of air power before the affects of the war drew to a close. The Russians had decided to try and starve the allies out of occupied Berlin; in effect Berlin had become an island for the allies in the sea of Communist occupation. The Allied Forces refused to leave. This resulted in the "Berlin Airlift", a massive operation involving the combined forces flying 2.5 million tons of food and supplies to the people of Berlin now totally cut off from the rest of the world.

The aircraft that General Dwight Eisenhower once described as one of the four weapons that most helped win the war was also the prominent workhorse during the Berlin airlift.

Used both by the USAAF and the RAF, the Douglas C47 was and perhaps still is, one of the world's best known and most loved aircraft. Known to the Americans as the Goony Bird and to the British as the Dakota it had been in use three years before the war and in some parts of the world its still in use today.

One pilot wrote when summing up the C47, "The Goony Bird protested, she rattled, she rolled and she leaked oil, she ran hot, she ran cold and she ran rough. On hot days it staggered along and scared you half to death, its wings flexing and twisting in a horrifying manner, it sank back to earth with a sigh of relief but she flew and flew and flew. The Goony Bird would take us wherever we had to go and brought us safely back home again, honest, faithful and magnificent machine that she was."

With the threat of atomic weapons being used by the Russians, it now became apparent to the Allied Air Forces that there would have to be major reconstructive action. In 1947 the United States Army Air Forces became the USAF, for both the RAF and the USAF much more advanced aircraft were needed. Aircraft that had served so well during the war years were now to be replaced by a new breed of machine and with that new machine came a new breed of pilot. This was the dawning of the jet age. Man was about to travel faster than ever before and before long, America was going to put that jet technology to the ultimate test in a new war with new rules.

APPENDIX 1
THE ROYAL AUXILIARY AIR FORCE

Most of us know a little about the RAF, but do you know about the 'The Royal Auxiliary Air Force' (known as the 'RAuxAF'). They seem perhaps to have been slightly forgotten for their role in the past, so they deservedly now, will be presented to you in short to give you an idea of their involvement. It originated many years ago through Lord Trenchard's vision of an elite corps of civilians who would serve their country in flying Squadrons in their spare time. Lord Trenchard was Winston Churchill's Chief Of Air Staff at the time and was able to institute an order in Council on 9th October 1924. The following year, the first Auxiliary Air Force squadrons known as the AAF were formed. By September 1939 there were 20 flying squadrons, equipped with a variety of operational aircraft that included Hurricanes, Spitfires and 47 balloon squadrons.

These AAF squadrons scored a high number of notable successes before and during World War II, check out what they have been up to.

- They destroyed the first German aircraft over British territorial waters and over the mainland.

- They destroyed the first U-Boat with the aid of airborne radar.

- The AAF achieved the first kill of a VI flying

bomb.

- They were the first to be equipped with jet-powered aircraft.

- They had the highest score of any British night fighter squadron.

In the Battle of Britain, the AAF provided 14 of the 62 squadrons in Fighter Command's Order of Battle and accounted for approximately 30% of the accredited enemy kills. The balloon squadrons also played their part, downing and deterring many hostile aircraft and were accredited with the destruction of 279 VI flying bombs.

These achievements were honoured by adding the prefix 'Royal' presented by King George VI in 1947. The regeneration of the RAuxAF began in 1979 when three Regiment Field squadrons, were formed. A Movement squadron was later formed in 1982, and following lessons learned during the war in the Falklands, an Aeromedical Evacuation squadron was also set up in 1983. A more recent addition, in 1987, was an auxiliary element named The Grampian Troop, which was formed within a regular RAF Regiment Rapier Air Defence squadron. A further step forward was taken in 1986, with the raising of four Defence Forces, with the role of ground defence of key points on air bases.

The award to the Service of its own badge marked the RAuxAF's Diamond Jubilee in 1984. This forms the basic motif of the Sovereign's Colour for the Royal Auxiliary Air Force, which was presented by the Queen in 1989. The words of the badge contain the motto 'COMITAMUR AD ASTRA' which translates to 'We go with them to the stars'.

During the Gulf War the Aeromedical and Movements squadrons performed with great merit in medical theatre and at other locations in the United Kingdom and overseas. Looking back at Lord Trenchard's vision we can see that it has been a truly justified achievement spanning 72 years. Meanwhile the Auxiliary concept has moved away from the provision of flying squadrons like that in World War II, the professional skill and enthusiasm of his young men in their twenties and thirties are matched by the men and women who constitute the RAuxAF of today.

APPENDIX 2
THE SECOND WORLD WAR

The second greatest global conflict that the world has seen was of course World War II. It was a result of the rise of tyrannical, militaristic regimes in Germany, Italy, and Japan, partly stemming from the Great Depression that swept over the world in the early 1930s and from the political environment created by the peace settlements following World War I.

After World War I defeated Germany, disappointed Italy, and ambitious Japan were anxious to regain and improve their force once again. All three countries had implemented forms of dictatorship which called for growth at the expense of their weaker neighbouring countries. They considered themselves as champions against Communism, thus gaining at least partial tolerance of their early actions from the more conservative democracies in the Western world. The desire for peace was of huge importance to these democracies and as a result left them unprepared for Military conflict.

'The League of Nations' a former international organisation; the forerunner to the United Nations was established by the peace treaties that ended World War I and was weakened from the start by the defection of the United States. The US were unable to promote disarmament and even more, the long economic depression fuelled national rivalries, increased fear and distrust. These factors made the people susceptible to the many false promises made to them by their leaders.

The failure of The League of Nations to stop the Second Sino-Japanese War in 1931 was followed by a rising upsurge of treaty violations and acts of aggression. Adolf Hitler, came to power in 1933, recreated the German army and prepared it for a war of conquest and domination. In 1936 he remilitarised the Rhineland. In the same period 1935 –1936 Benito Mussolini conquered Ethiopia for Italy; and from 1936 to 1939 the Spanish civil war raged on whilst Germany and Italy helped the fascist forces of Francisco Franco to victory. In March 1938 Germany seized Austria, and in September that year the British and French policy of appeasement toward the Axis (coalition of countries headed by Germany, Italy, and Japan) reached its height with the loss of Czechoslovakia to Germany.

When Germany occupied Czechoslovakia in March 1939 and when Italy seized Albania in April 1939, Great Britain and France abandoned their policy of appeasement and set about creating an "anti aggression" front that included alliances with Turkey, Greece, Romania, and Poland. In May 1939 Germany and Italy signed a full military alliance. Months later the Soviet-German non-aggression pact was signed which removed German fear of a possible two-front war; Germany was ready to launch an attack on Poland.

World War II began on September 1, 1939, when Germany, without a declaration of war, invaded Poland. Britain and France declared war on Germany on September 3, all the members of the Commonwealth of Nations, except Ireland, rapidly followed suit. The fighting in Poland was fairly brief. The German blitzkrieg (lightening war) with its new techniques of mechanised and air warfare, crushed the Polish defences. The conquest was almost complete when Soviet forces entered East Poland on 17 September. The campaign ended with the partition of Poland and whilst the USSR defeated Finland in the Finnish-Russian War during 1939 - 1940 the British and the French spent an inactive winter blockading Germany by sea.

This relatively inactive period ended with the surprise invasion on April 9 1940 of Denmark and Norway by the Germans. Denmark offered no resistance at all and Norway was conquered by June 9. On May 10, German forces overran Luxembourg and invaded Holland and Belgium. On May 13 they outflanked the Maginot Line. Their forces raced to the English Channel to cut off Flanders and continue their advance through Europe, allied forces were forced to evacuate Dunkirk between May 26 and June 4. General Weygand had replaced General Gamelin as supreme Allied commander, but was unable to halt the Allied fiasco in France (Battle of France). On June 22, France signed an armistice with Germany, followed by an armistice with Italy, which had entered the war on June 10. The Vichy government was set up in France under Marshal Pétain. Britain was the only remaining Allied power that resisted, under the inspiring leadership of Winston Churchill. Of course the Germans did not like this and attempted to bomb England into submission. So begun the 'Battle of Britain'.

Whilst Germany was receiving its first setback in the 'Battle of Britain' fought entirely in the air, the theatre of war was broadened by the Italian attack on the British in North Africa, by the Italian invasion on the October 28 1940 of Greece, and by German submarine warfare in the Atlantic Ocean. Bulgaria, Hungary and Romania joined the Axis in the latter part of 1940, but Yugoslavia defied German pressure, and on April 6 1941, Germany launched attacks on Yugoslavia and Greece, The Germans were victorious with Crete soon to follow the next month. Great Britain gained a new ally on June 22 1941. Germany joined by Italy, Romania, Hungary, Slovakia, and Finland invaded the Soviet Union. By December 1941 German divisions had destroyed a substantial part of the Soviet army and had swamped much of European Russia. However, the harsh Russian winter halted the German sweep, and the push to Moscow was foiled by a Soviet counter offensive.

The United States wanted to remain in more of a neutral position but it did not take long before they were gradually drawn closer to the war by the force of events. They wanted to help Britain so

Congress voted and lend-leased aid early in 1941. In August 1941 President Franklin Roosevelt met Churchill on the high seas and together they formulated the 'Atlantic Charter', a general statement of democratic aims. To establish bases to protect it's shipping from attacks by German submarines, the United States occupied Greenland in April 1941 and later shared the occupation of Iceland; relations with Germany became increasingly strained as the attacks continued despite warnings. The aggressive acts of Japan in China, Indochina, and Thailand provoked disapproval and disgust from the United States.

Efforts to reach a peaceful settlement were crushed on Dec 7 1941 when Japan without warning attacked Pearl Harbour, the Philippines, and Malaya. The US, the Commonwealth of Nations and Holland, declared war on Japan. A few days later Germany and Italy declared war on the United States. The first phase of the war in the Pacific was disastrous for the Allies. Japan quickly conquered the Philippines, Malaya, Burma, Indonesia and many other Pacific islands. By the middle of 1942, Japan had advanced to the Aleutian Islands and New Guinea. Australia became the chief Allied base for the countermoves against Japan. The first Allied naval successes against Japan were scored in the battles of the Coral Sea and Midway, where American bombers eradicated the major part of Japan's carrier fleet and forced Japan into retreat. Midway was the first crucial blow against the Axis by Allied forces. On the land the Allies took the offensive and arrived in New Guinea on August 7 1942 on Guadalcanal in the Solomon Islands.

Despite the improved position in the Pacific, the late summer of 1942 was perhaps the darkest period of the war for the Allies. In North Africa, the Axis forces under Field Marshal Rommel were sweeping into Egypt; they also penetrated the Caucasus in Russia and launched a massive offensive against Stalingrad. In the Atlantic, even to the shores of the United States and in the Gulf of Mexico, German submarines were sinking Allied shipping at an alarming rate. Yet the Axis war machine showed signs of tiredness and in October 1942 Britain's General Montgomery pounded Rommel at Al Alamein in North Africa. This was followed by the American invasion of Algeria on 8 November. General de Gaulle sent his Free French forces to join the Americans and the British alongside the regular French forces that had passed to the Allies after the surrender of Admiral Darlan. Tunisia, North Africa was cleared of Axis forces by May 1943 after heavy fighting.

Around the same time the Soviet counter offensive at Stalingrad resulted in the surrender of the German 6th Army, nearly constant Russian advances followed this. In the Mediterranean the Allies followed up their African victory by conquering Sicily in August 1943. The invasion of Italy began and finished within a month with the Italians surrendering to Allied Forces on 8 September. It wasn't quite over as the German army in Italy fought fiercely, Rome finally fell on 4 June 1944 after the battles of Monte Cassino and Anzio. The submarine threat in the Atlantic had virtually ended by the summer of 1944. Throughout German-occupied Europe, the Resistance and underground forces that were largely supplied by the Allies began to wage war against their oppressors.

The invasion of German-held France led by General Eisenhower was decided upon at the Casablanca Conference where the Allied forces pledged to continue the war until the unconditional surrender of Axis forces. By the beginning of 1944 air warfare had turned overwhelmingly in favour of the Allied forces as they pounded German industry and infrastructure, This air offensive led the way for the first landing of the Allied troops in Northern France on June 6 1944. A second landing took place on August 15 in the South of France. After heavy fighting in Normandy, Allied armoured divisions forged their way to the Rhine, clearing most of France and Belgium of German forces by October 1944.

On the Eastern Front at around the same time, the Soviet armies were doing extremely well and were sweeping through the Baltic States, East Poland, Byelorussia and the Ukraine, which in turn forced the surrender of Romania, Finland and Bulgaria. Having evacuated the Balkan Peninsula, the Germans held Hungary until February 1945, but Germany itself was under huge pressure.

On March 7, the Western Allies chief commanders Omar Bradley and General Montgomery crossed the Rhine after having smashed through the strongly fortified Siegfried Line. The collapse of Germany came after the meeting on April 25 where the Western and Russian armies met at Torgau in Saxony, and to the news of Hitler's death and the ruins of Berlin which were falling to the Russians. The unconditional surrender of Germany was signed at Reims on May 7 and was sanctioned at Berlin on May 8.

Prior to the surrender of Germany and after the completion of the campaigns in the Solomon Islands and New Guinea during 1943 and 1944, the Allied advance moved relentlessly, in two lines that met Japan through scattered island groups, those being the Philippines, the Mariana Islands, Okinawa, and Iwo Jima in Japan. Japan still refused to surrender even after the Allied appeal made at the Potsdam Conference. On August 6 1945, the United States used the atomic bomb for the first time and devastated Hiroshima. Three days later on August 9, the second bomb was dropped on Nagasaki. The USSR had already invaded Manchuria and on August 14, Japan finally announced its surrender, formally signed aboard the U.S. battleship 'Missouri' in Tokyo Bay on September 2 1945.

ACKNOWLEDGEMENTS

I would like to thank the following for their part in making this book possible:

The United States Navy
The United States Air Force
Ministry of Defence
Imperial War Museum
The National Museum of Naval Aviation
RAF Museum, Hendon
Westland Helicopters
McDonnell Douglas Aircraft Corporation
British Aerospace
Vickers
Rolls Royce
Historic Footage Ltd
Sarah Merrill
Steve Connor
Julian Ankersmit
Annekin Wild
Phin Hall
Robert Garofalo

Cover picture by Corbis
Artwork by Stuart Forrester

If you have enjoyed this book, please consider reviewing it on Amazon or Goodreads (or both)

And feel free visit the *Flying Machine And Their Heroes* website for other titles in this series and to receive a free audiobook:

flyingmachinesandtheirheroes.com

www.ingramcontent.com/pod-product-compliance
Lightning Source LLC
Chambersburg PA
CBHW072014060426
42446CB00043B/2545